Mr. Uraly's Italy

A book by RL Lane

My book journey started with DAW and went nowhere with DAW, but I found Peter...

"Dear Peter,

Welcome to **EcarreI**. A world where everyone cares...

Why did I have to create it in a fiction fantasy world..."

That is what Peter first read when he opened the box that contained the first series of my life. Peter…

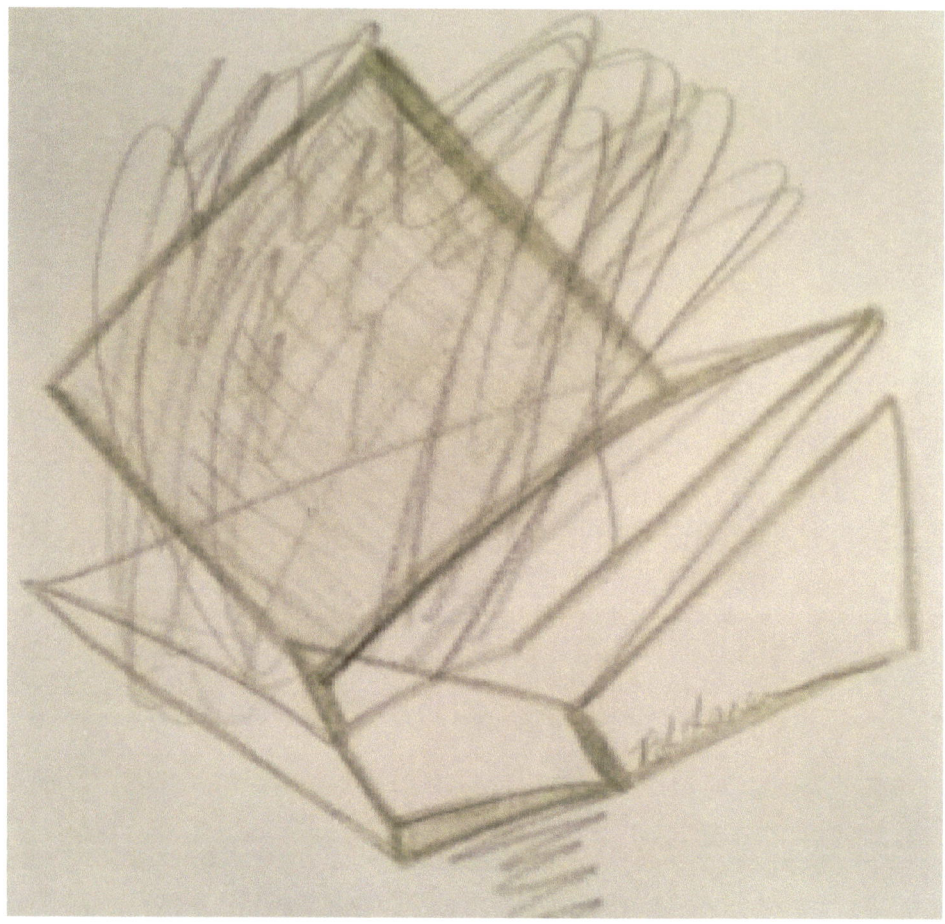

9:19am: Atelboro. That means something. Is that in Texas? No! Attleboro is in Massachusetts. Is that where the research place is located? I know it is in MA somewhere. I looked online. There is a historic train station there and it was once known as "The Jewelry Capital of the World". I looked up points of interest. There are four museums there. Wait! Is this where Mary Todd Lincoln's missing jewelry pieces are? Can someone who works at these museums please let me know if you have on display Mary Todd Lincoln's earrings, brooch, and bracelet that she wore at the inauguration? I think the necklace is still on display in the Museum of Fine Arts Boston.

Somehow I hit something and my page went to fraternity and sorority jewelry. That's funny, I was just texting someone about the Greek fraternities. I was warning her about them, but I was only kidding and she was talking about the food anyway. Greek food.

One of them must like dirt like me. One of them clearly has a dirty mind. I am not even going to guess which one…

1:39am: I think Mr. King beli ves there are things that cannot be explained. If I ever get to meet him, we can talk about the beginning of his book journey…

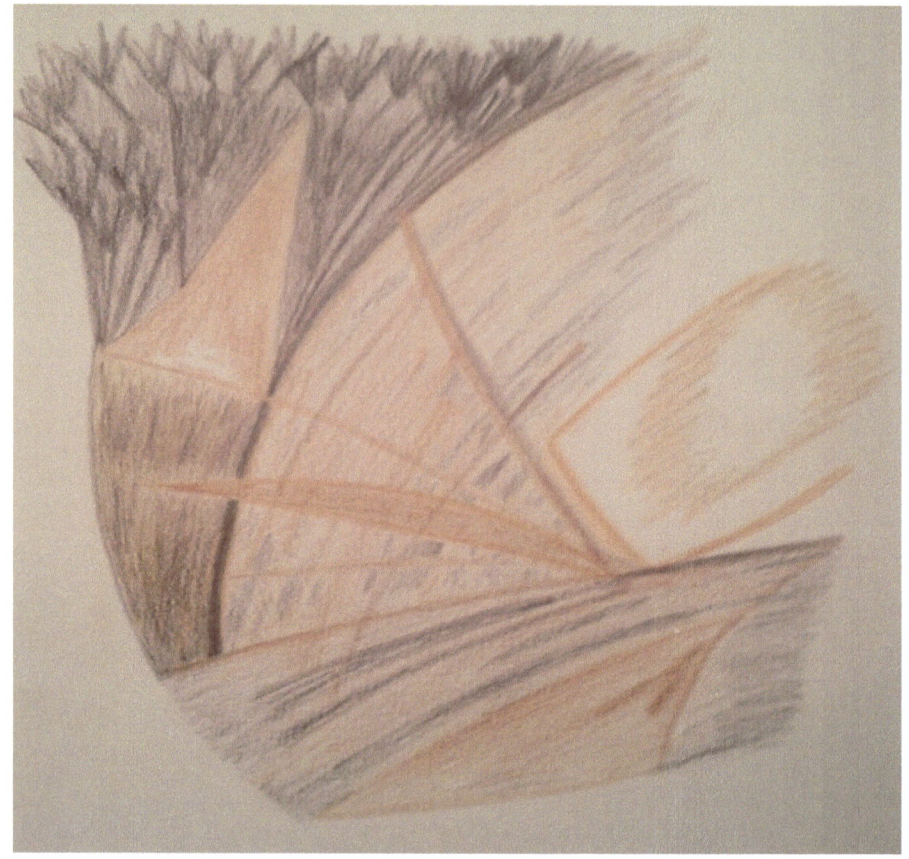

We can RA…right an…sonething. We are supposed to write soneting together? A sonnet! *A poetic form that originated in Italy. Of course…where my ancestors are from. That is our connection. We like pos…pos…poems. Pos pos? Is that a thing? I have ancestors in Italy. We will write a sonnet which started in Italy. No! Our poem will start in Italy! "On the streets of Italy…" I already got us started. I could meet you in Italy if that is easier than Maine because I have never been to Uraly…Italy…and if you can buy me a ticket and a pls…r…t…place to stay I will be happy to Take the time to meet you here…there! Please R T? Who's Arty? Mr. King, do you have a butler? Uraly? I think that is a made up Place…*

On the streets of Italy, a man
Mr. Uraly…

There! Now we have almost 2 lines of our poem. I really do think we should be on his streets of Italy to properly be able to tell his story. Can we call our poem "Your Rally" or "Your Rally's Italy"? It really was because of my rally…where they all rallied to help me that got me to this book world so that I could write to you. I hope Mr. Urali…oh no…it's Mr. Uralli will let us know if we get his poem write. The one from Lon…Lombardy, Italy…he may be in London now.

I don't know…the time changed to 9:28pm because I hit a key by mistake when I was reading this from my phone notes to put it in my book document. I am just noting it in case it means something in the future…

I don't know much about you
And you know nothing about me…
But we can talk about words
How they can be smithed
Or smothered in love
How they can give colour
To a clear sky
How they can say Hi
When you are too shy
How they can say Goodbye
When you have to fly

How words can be so empty
Ow…Ouch
Or they can mean the world…
Touch every single person they meet.

I think you secretly like poetry. It would not really be fir…

Xchange their lives as they cross paths.

    Wait! You do like poems! I looked online. Perhaps you like it more than tour…your fans realize. Wait? Do you tour? I think I have already written more poems than you, but that is partially in rebellion against the no poems that DAW said. Wait! Maine was just a message yesterday. I will drive there to see you. Please email me at RosaLeeeLane@gmail.com...

I'll check every day so I do not miss it and can respond right away with the days I am available. I do not think my schedule is as busy as yours, so I think we will be able to find a date. Maybe you were the ban…man I saw by the Rick…rock. Oh no, that was Rick. He is already dead. You are not. I promise I will not chop you up on s…in a little box and secretly Hug…hide you away. I am not obsessed with you,

But I would like to hug you that is tru.

Because I do like to touch people.
They don't seem to mind.

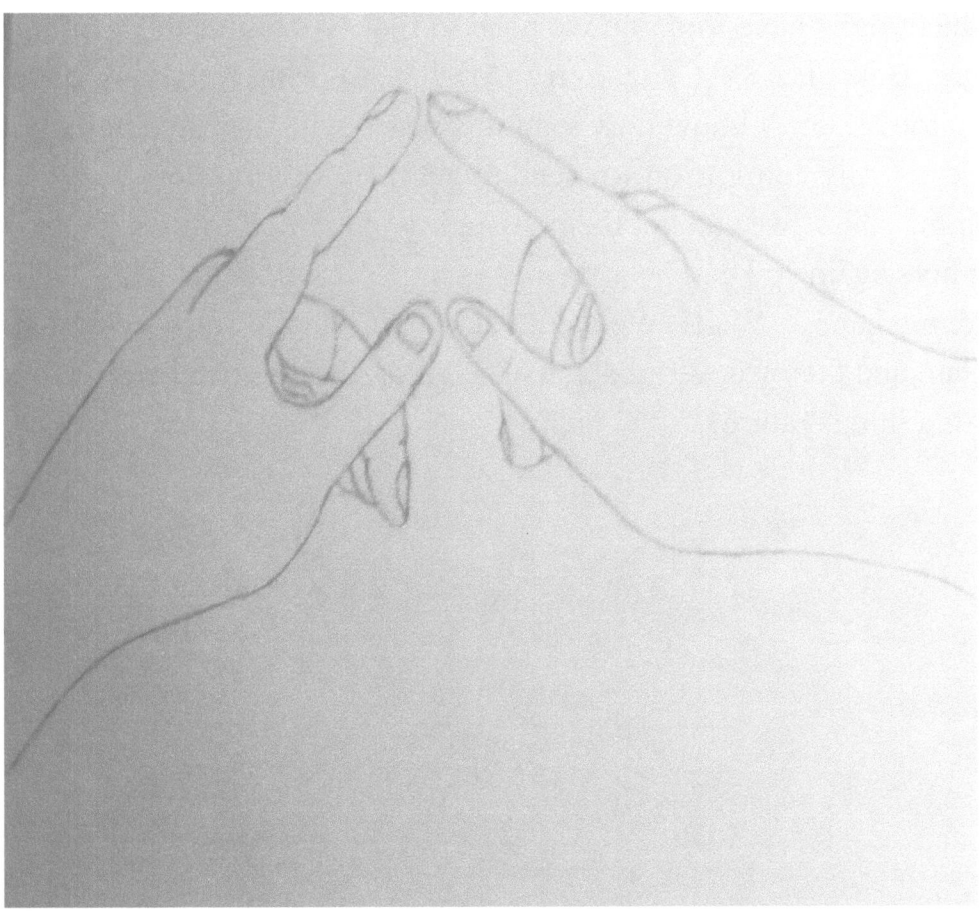

Perhaps you can help me to not write so many endings to my books in my series and how to not write my books while I am half asleep. Look how many typos we have. I really did used to like my sleep. I am only 44. I have to keep this body running, plus I like to do experiments on it...the chemical ones because everyone says my body has to stay here, so I have limited time to finish my experiments...the chemical ones. I am sure you will agree if you never experiment...try anything different...you...

1:37am. You might invent something. I want to invent something. A tally...actually I want up...to invent a lot of thingsxxx...the fixes to all my problems. The band aids to cross those wounds. I need to tally up all the things I have told you we need to fix. Of course, those church bellaz. Bells in AZ? Can you try, Arizona, to bring back your church bells, too? I don't know how long this peace will last, especially if a battle is really coming, so we need to get them ringing now. My Momma said if we can get them swinging in the bell towers, she will ring hers again so I can hear them this time. Loud and clear. That will make me happy. Wait! We went back in time! We were writing at 1:39am and then we went back to 1:37am! Another trip back in time is coming in our future...

Another crack in time as we roll along

Squeeze those handlebars

Hold on tight

Ring the bell

Loud and clear

Here we come…

Why do so many of my poems look like wine stoppers? Is there a party in our future?

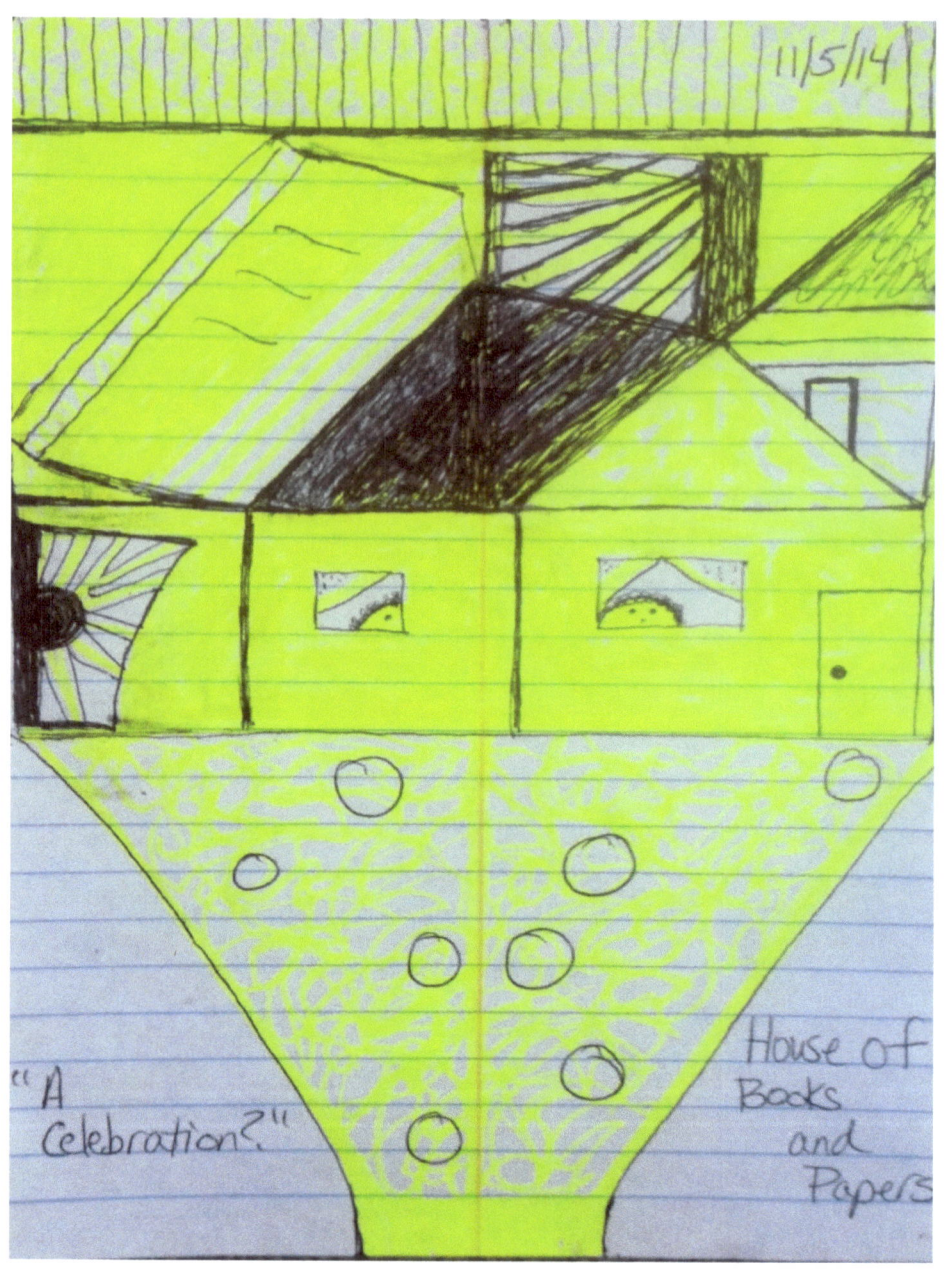

11/5/14

"A Celebration?"

House of Books and Papers

1:43am: Mr. King, it has been a pleasure writing words to you. I hope you don't think it is creepy that I was thinking of you in the middle of the night…

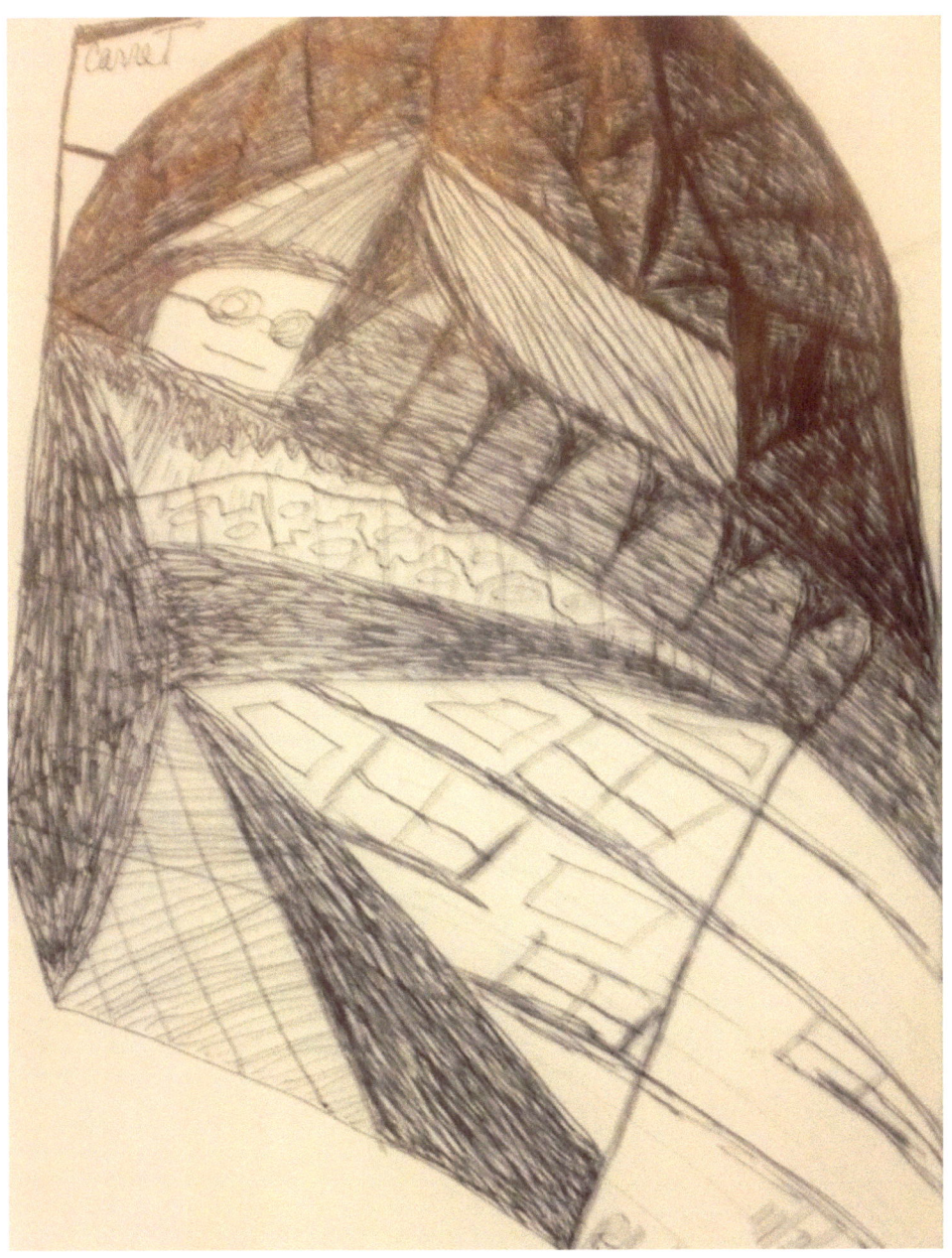

Wait! Are you married? We have that in common if you are. That could be our connection for today, but it will not be in six days. I will not be married after that. If you promise to not chop me up, I will promise to not chop you up. That will be our pact. I do keep my promises and I really would like to meet you and speak to you and I do hope you have a sense of humor.

Lock the bedroom door! (read it quietly and slowly and creepily)

Lock the bedroom door! (read it quietly and slowly and creepily)

10:11am. Peter, you too. I am hoping for that sense of humor. I've written about you do…so much I am starting to love you. I do hope your wife doesn't mind. I realized it was her…the message of Betsy back in "Chapel Street Signs"…that was her. I have no doubt because that is when Don and Elsie first started ad ding…sending me messages and I have no doubt they loved your wife, and I think they are counting on us to get this write…right. Wait! I just checked. There was no Betsy in Chapel Street. That is odd. I thought there was. Wait! There is one though in "secret Life OV an antE". I am glad.

I think Henry helped me write the letter to Mr. King…

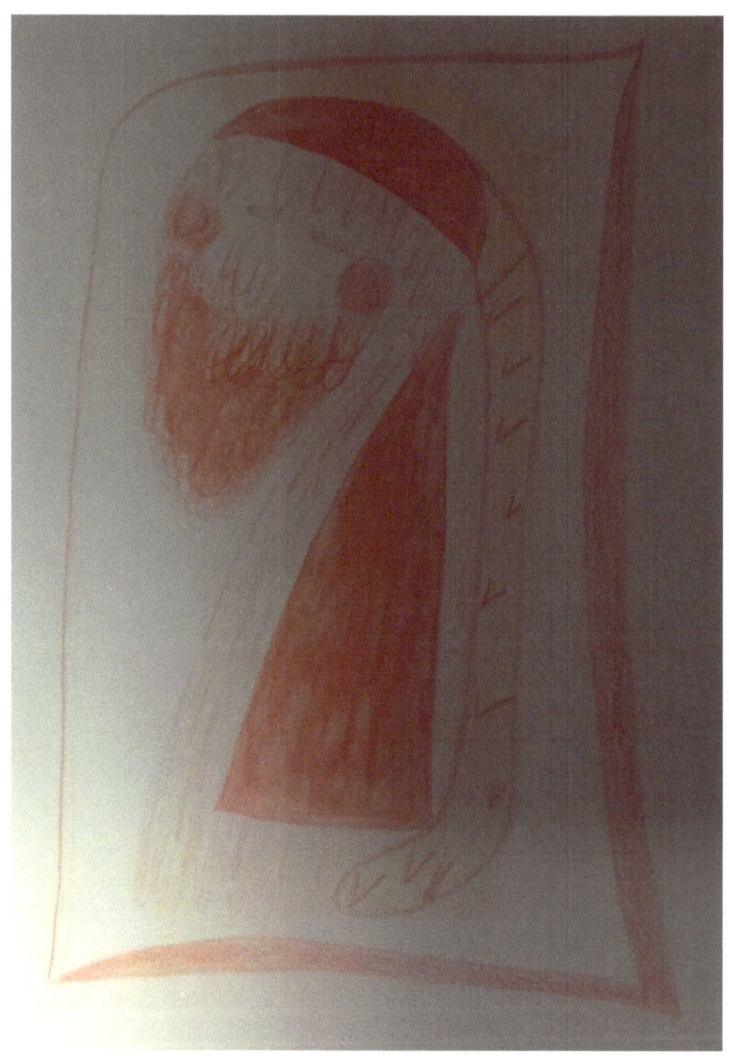

Ham! The food pantries in NY, a squirrel with acorns (he was mad, he thought the cast…cats were going to take his dinner), something with those museums, schools, children, the firemen…we have to help them all in some way. With these books. Oh, and with the movies. I don't think we have to really help the squirrels. I think my Dad was just getting mad that I kept forgetting to say we need to help those food pantries feed the hungry. We will. Actually, Mr. King, I think that was wrong. I think I wrote that letter to you myself. I made a mistake. I am human after all. Wait! Why aren't we supposed to help the Navy? The Army? The Marines? That doesn't make sense. Oh. They say they are ok. They say there are other organizations that need our help more…plus something tells me the military would not be fans of the unexplained. Their rules are not open to interpretation. They are just simply the rules that the soldiers follow…so they can get back home safely…

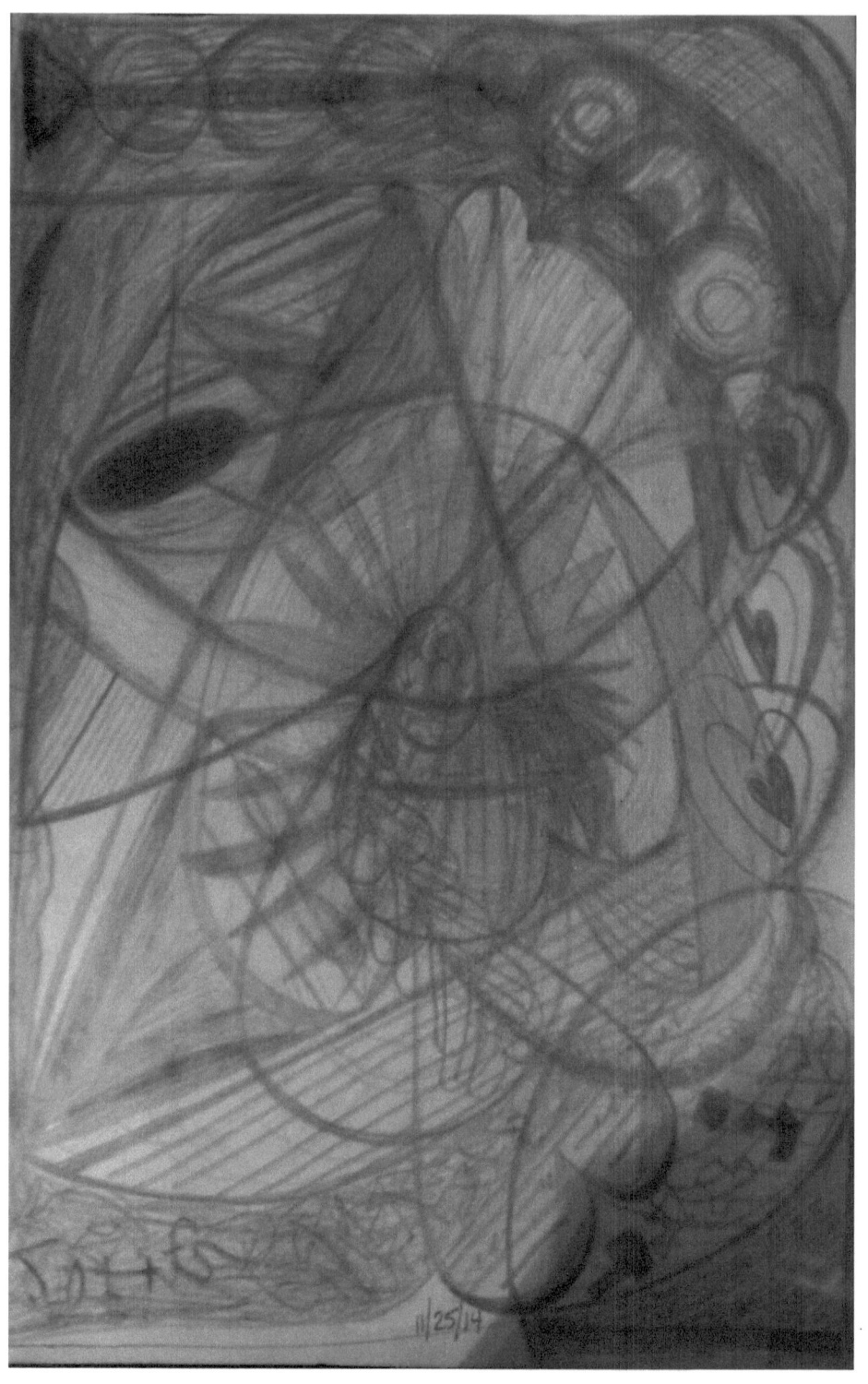

I looked up. The clock had stopped at exactly 1:03. Why? I looked in the books for that time…1:03. Nothing. Except part of this…

11:03am. I can see them all sitting around the table talking about CSS.

Oh wait, it's at 1:03 and a half. Oh wait. It hasn't stopped. The clock is running. I wonder why.

Mass. I just made it for the end. I wonder why. I went to class with my little 4th graders. I was driving home and then I thought of the farm. I wonder why. I thought I would drive out to the farm and get a doughnut. I got there and did get a doughnut on a beautiful fall day. I was going to leave and turn right to go home, but instead I went straight…

"Chittinango" –

Where the sun shines out

...the second part of my trip that day was to a small village, but it was for my...me because I knew that entire area meant something to her that I needed to know. I followed the road down a route. I followed that road not really knowing what I was looking for...

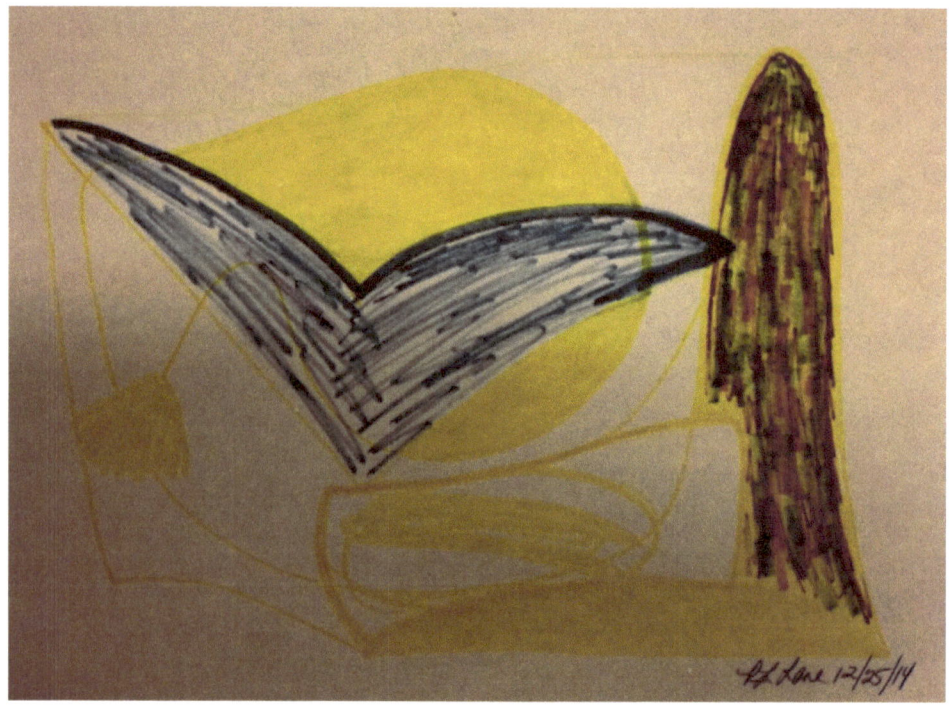

...and turned a curve and saw the beautiful autumn day. I realized how pretty the road was. It must remind her of something. Oh. That's it. It reminds her of the falls she loved. Apples and pumpkins and peaches. The Doctor's wife...

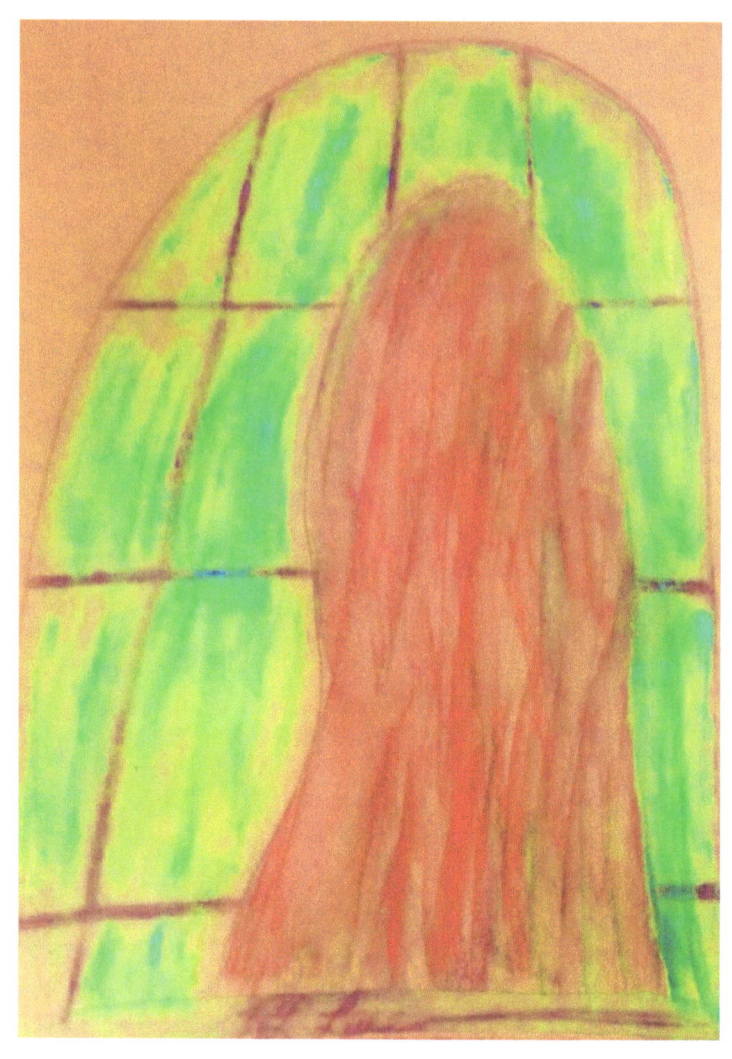

In loving memory

Of the Doctor and the Rose

About the Author and *Illustrator*

RL Lane has published the EcarreT series and a collection of art books featuring the illustrations throughout the books. The series begins with "Chapel Street Signs"…

…unexplained connections that challenge us to beli ve. A woman, a Dad a Doctor, a cat and mouse, a horse and tale tell their stories. "Do you beli ve in spirits?" I asked my friend. "Well look", he said, "I believe there are things that cannot be explained…" Oh. Plus, hear ov a Mom's battle with her struggle to connect to the woman…her little girl.

Welcome to EcarreT…a world
Where everyone cares
Why did I have to create it in…

A fiction fantasy world?

You may already know why, but you will see regardless of what you believe as a girl's journey of love and faith on her "Touring Machine" take her on the best journey of her mundane life. A life well on its way takes a turn in a direction that could've never been seen or even dreamed…

The author can be contacted at:

RosaLeeeLane@gmail.com
www.Amazon.com/author/readrllane

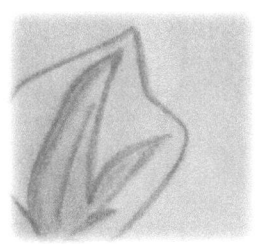

www.ingramcontent.com/pod-product-compliance
Lightning Source LLC
Chambersburg PA
CBHW050433180526
45159CB00006B/2513